Brain

DOUGLAS MATHERS

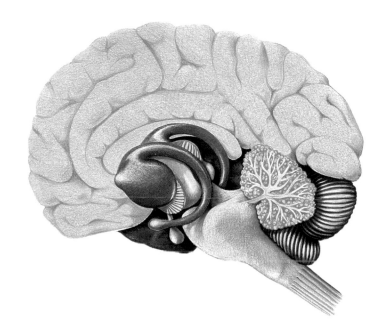

illustrated by
ANDREW FARMER and **ROBINA GREEN**

Troll Associates

Library of Congress Cataloging-in-Publication Data

Mathers, Douglas.
    Brain / by Douglas Mathers; illustrated by Andrew Farmer &
Robina Green.
        p.   cm.
    Summary: Describes the brain, its parts, and functions, and
discusses how it communicates with other parts of the body.
    ISBN 0-8167-2090-8 (lib. bdg.)   ISBN 0-8167-2091-6 (pbk.)
    1. Brain—Juvenile literature.   2. Neurophysiology—Juvenile
literature. [1. Brain.   2. Nervous system.]   I. Farmer, Andrew,
ill. II. Green, Robina, ill.   III. Title.
QP376.M38   1992
612.8'2—dc20   90-42883

Published by Troll Associates.

Edited by Neil Morris
Designed by COOPER-WILSON
Picture research by Jan Croot

Printed in the U.S.A.

10 9 8 7 6 5 4 3 2 1

Illustrators
Andrew Farmer front and back cover, pp 1, 2-3, 4-5,
    9, 10-11, 13, 14, 14-15, 20 (bottom)
Robina Green front cover, pp 5, 12, 17, 20 (top), 23,
    25, 26, 27, 29
Additional illustrations by COOPER-WILSON

Picture credits:
Barnaby's 18 (left)
Bridgeman Art Library 29
Luke Hamilton 17
Dr. Ian Harvey (Institute of Neurology, London) 8
Netherlands Office for Fine Arts 18 (right)
Science Photo Library (CNRI) front cover,
    (US National Institutes of Health) 7, (CNRI) 16
ZEFA 21

Acknowledgement:
Routledge and Princeton University Press for the
    extract from *Collected Works of C.G. Jung* on page 25.

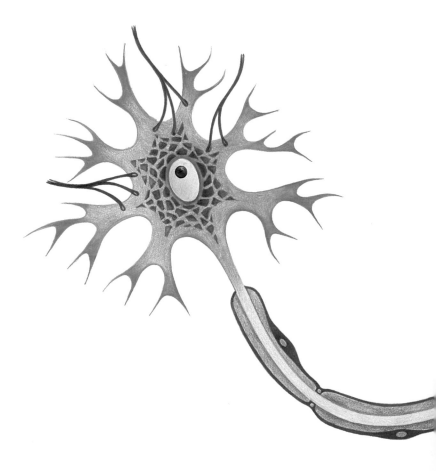

Contents

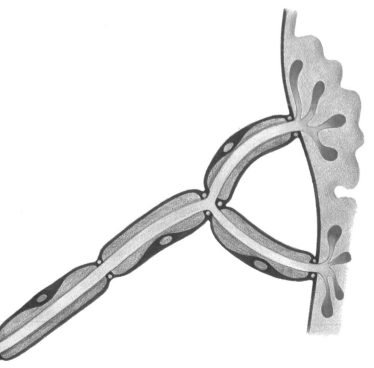

What does the brain do?

Why do you feel happy or sad, hurt or afraid? How do you think, learn, or talk? How do you breathe, see, or move? Think of anything you can do. Whatever it is, you could not do it without your brain.

The adult brain is roughly the size of a coconut, and is probably more complex than anything else in the universe. A mature brain contains at least twelve billion nerve *cells* – more cells than the number of stars visible from Earth with the most powerful telescope.

▼ Your brain is inside your skull, connected to the spinal cord inside your backbone. Together they form the central nervous system. Nerves run from the spinal cord all over the body.

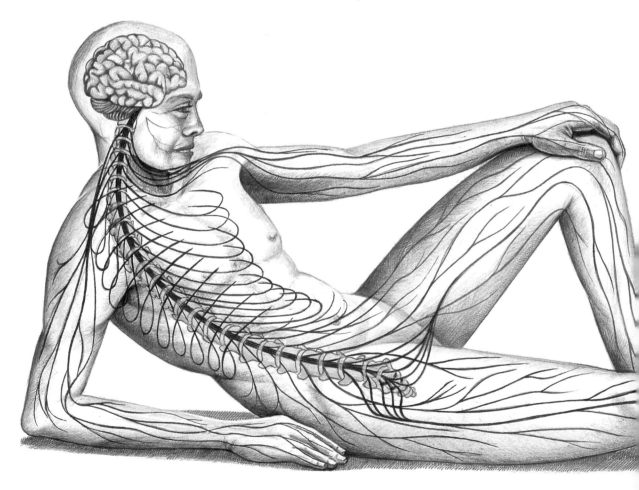

Your brain connects with your *spinal cord*, and together they make up your body's *central nervous system. Nerves* branch off from the spinal cord, connecting it to every part of your body. These nerves carry instructions from your brain to your body, and messages from your sense organs to your brain. Like a telephone switchboard operator, your brain monitors all these signals. But the brain is much more than a switchboard. If all the world's telephone networks were made of brain cells, they would use less brain area than the size of a pea!

Brains are often compared to computers, but a computer is just a very fast calculator that uses electricity. The brain actually produces almost enough electricity to light a flashlight bulb, and it has a limitless ability to learn new skills. Each brain cell can be linked to any other one. The number of possible link-ups is so great that, if printed, it would cover a piece of paper that stretched to the Moon and back – twelve times!

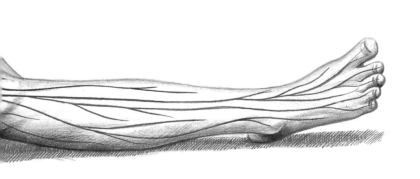

▲ The brain is involved in all our actions. When juggling, we use our eyes and hands. Our brain judges speed and movement. Actions that need thinking about are called conscious acts.

Other actions are unconscious. A reflex in the spinal cord pulls your hand away from something very hot. Your brain instructs your hand to scratch. Usually we do this "without thinking."

Historical ideas about the brain

For thousands of years, people have tried to understand the brain, but today we still have much to learn. To understand how a machine works, we usually dismantle it. But brains are almost impossible to take apart. The outside of the brain gives few clues as to how the inside works.

Prehistoric man had some idea that the skull was connected with illness. Skulls have been found with holes deliberately made in them, probably to let out demons or spirits. 5,000 years ago, doctors in Egypt noticed that soldiers injured at the back of the head often went blind. They also observed that injuries to the left side of the brain paralyzed the right side of the body, and the other way around. They guessed that the brain made movements happen, but they believed the liver contained our mind and soul.

When ancient Greeks looked inside the brains of dead people, they saw hollow spaces filled with air. They thought that air mixed with blood to make memories. In the Middle Ages, people believed that our emotions came from the mixing of four elements (fire, water, earth, and air) in the body. The elements supposedly appeared as fluids called "humors." These fluids were thought to cause hot temper, misery, optimism, and calmness.

▼People used to believe that bumps on the skull described skills and character. This is a so-called phrenological map. (1) form (2) size (3) individuality (4) predicting (5) comparison (6) human nature (7) kindness (8) worship (9) firmness (10) self-esteem (11) continuity (12) home-loving (13) parental love (14) weight (15) locality (16) causes (17) agreeableness (18) imitation (19) spirituality (20) hope (21) conscience (22) pleasure (23) friendship (24) marriage (25) color (26) time (27) gaiety (28) ideals (29) cunning (30) caution (31) fighting (32) order (33) tune (34) constructiveness (35) greed (36) secrets (37) hunger (38) destructiveness (39) vitality.

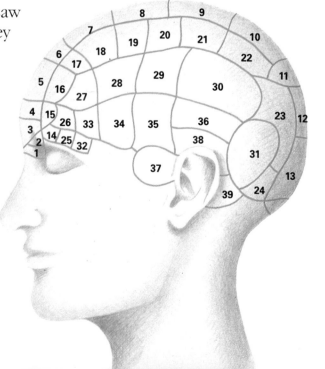

Over the centuries, scientists have studied the brain. Like the Egyptian doctors, they have tried to find links between damage to particular parts of the brain and loss of certain body functions.

Scientists began to build a picture of which part of the brain controls what. In the nineteenth century, doctors tried to draw this information as maps of the brain. The idea was a good one, but the maps were very inaccurate. Today scientists use electronic scanners on living subjects to gain a better understanding of the brain and to make much better maps.

▲ The "humors," as drawn in the Middle Ages. *From left to right:* hot temper, misery, optimism, and calmness.

▼ These modern pictures, called PET scans, show images of a diseased brain (*left*) and a healthy brain (*right*).

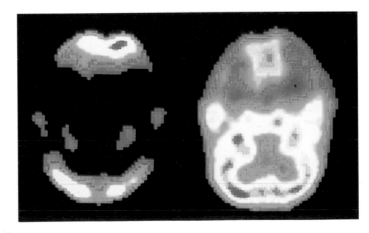

The brain in the body

Your brain fills most of the top half of your head. Positioned above the eyes and between the ears, it extends down at the back to connect with the spinal cord. At the front it is linked to your eyes and nose.

The brain sits above the largest *blood vessels* leading from the heart, like a ball balanced on a fountain. The blood vessels supply the brain with the food and oxygen it needs. The brain receives about 33 quarts (35 liters) of blood each hour. Our survival depends on the brain working properly. If food is scarce, the rest of the body will do without it in order to keep the brain going.

The brain is so important that it must be well protected. The tough bone of the skull acts as armor for the brain. Skulls are rounded for additional strength.

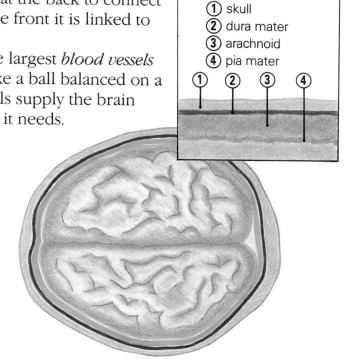

▼ The coverings of the brain:
① skull
② dura mater
③ arachnoid
④ pia mater

① ② ③ ④

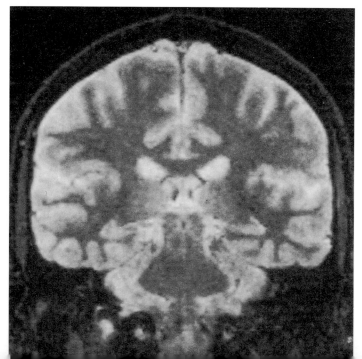

► This picture is an NMR scan. The skull looks like a white helmet. The fluid appears black, and the layers of the upper brain are white and gray.

8

Three layers of skinlike *membranes*, called the *meninges*, completely cover the brain to provide further protection. A leathery outer layer (the *dura mater*) surrounds the spongy *arachnoid*, which is filled with a special liquid. This protects the brain from shocks and helps to supply it with food. Beneath the arachnoid, another fine membrane, the *pia mater*, follows every wrinkle on the brain's surface. Spaces inside the brain are also filled with liquid, so that the brain's soft tissues do not get disturbed as you move your head.

The spinal cord is an extension of the brain that runs down the middle of your back. It needs flexible protection, which is provided by the spinal column, and by the same tough coverings and fluid as the brain. Nerves run out from the spinal cord to give instructions to all parts of the body. Other nerves run back to the spinal cord to tell the brain what is happening in and around your body.

▼ The spinal cord (**1**), seen here as it runs behind your chest. The bundle of nerves it contains mainly come from the motor area or go to the sensory area of the upper brain. Nerves (**2**) run between the segments of the backbone (**3**). Special nerve branches join together beside the spine (**4**). These communicate with the lower brain and control the body's internal workings, such as breathing and digestion.

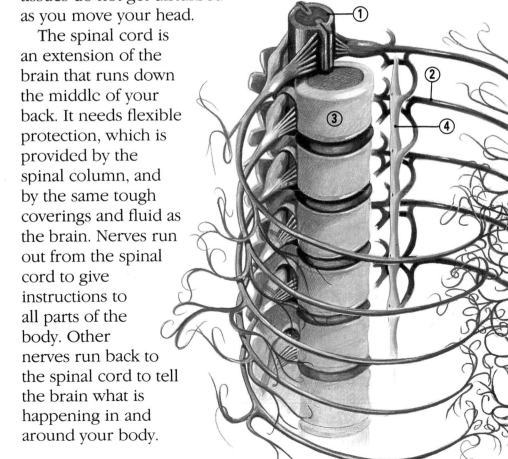

What the brain is made of

Like almost all living things, the brain is made of cells. Cells are the basic unit of life.
Most cells have three main parts – the *cell membrane*, the *cytoplasm*, and the *nucleus*. The membrane is the outer surface of the cell. Anything entering or leaving the cell must pass through it. Water, salts, oxygen, and food enter, while waste substances leave. The cytoplasm is the area of chemical processing, where energy is made. Near the center of the cell is the nucleus. This controls the chemicals the cell makes and directs its growth.

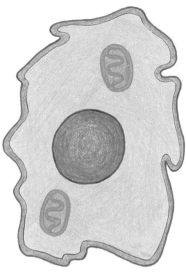

▲ A cell, showing its nucleus near the center. We can also see two energy-making structures, called *mitochondria*.

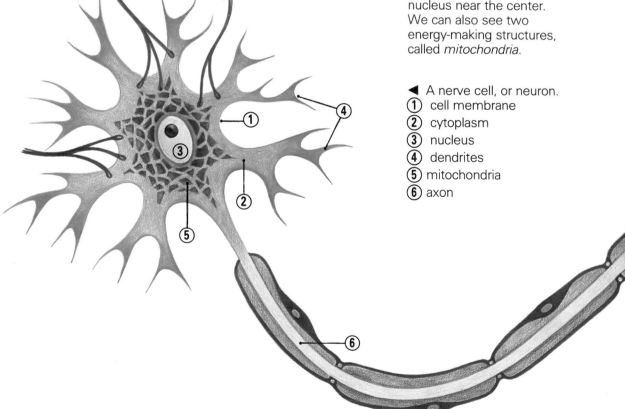

◄ A nerve cell, or neuron.
① cell membrane
② cytoplasm
③ nucleus
④ dendrites
⑤ mitochondria
⑥ axon

► Neurons come in more shapes and sizes than any other cell in your body. They never work alone. Each neuron is like a tree in a forest. It is part of a network, made up of as many neurons as a forest has trees. For example: the red tree could be neurons making finger muscles move; the blue tree could be neurons sensing what the fingers touch; and the green tree could be neurons controlling blood flow in the fingers.

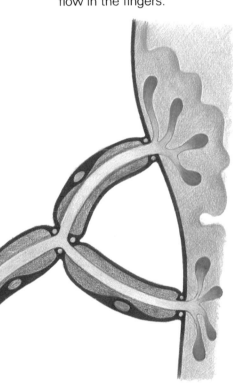

The brain is made of three main types of cells. Most important are the nerve cells, or *neurons*. These are the electrically active chemical factories that do our thinking. They are found mainly in the upper part of the brain. Packed around the neurons are *glia*, which support and feed the neurons. A third type of cells, the *macrophages*, clear up dead cells and kill germs.

Unlike other cells in our body, neurons do not divide to make new cells. But they do grow and make new connections to other neurons. Brain cells actually die at a rate of about one million a day! You need not worry, because we have enough to live beyond a hundred.

Neurons look like trees in a forest. Branches called *dendrites* spread out from the neurons to carry signals to and from other nearby neurons. Neurons pass messages through *axons*, which can be as long as your body. Axons travel out into the body like roots to make muscles work, or go to distant parts of the brain.

11

How brain cells pass messages

Brain cells form networks to take in and communicate information. One network receives information from the body and the outside world. A second network puts this information together into patterns. A third network recognizes patterns and decides what to do about them.

The place where two brain cells touch is called a *synapse*. When one cell has a message for another, it sends a packet of chemicals across the synapse to it. Each cell gets lots of these packets at any one time. When it receives enough packets of chemicals, the cell sends an electrical signal down its axon. This might, for example, cause the muscles in your big toe to twitch.

Messages from the brain to the body leave from the bottom part of the brain via the axons. Axons are covered in *myelin*, which is a fatty material that stops the electrical message from leaking out of the axon.

Brain cells also send other types of chemical packets. These stop electrical messages from being sent anywhere. The brain spends more time switching messages off than on. Look at this page. Much of it is white. If it were completely covered in letters, we wouldn't be able to read any of the words. In the same way, if all our brain cells worked at once, we wouldn't be able to understand what any of them were saying.

▲ A synapse. Packets of chemicals fit into special holes, like a key in a lock.

▼ The longest nerves in your body are those from your brain to your big toe and back again. Sensory nerves tell the brain where the toe is, how hot it is, and what it is standing on. Motor nerves make the toe move.

▼Brain cells grow in layers to form networks. Pyramidal cells (**1**) send signals to move muscles. Star cells (**2**) tell the brain that the muscle is moving. Some connecting cells (**3**) go to the part of the brain controlling movement and balance.

Neurons can only pass basic "on" or "off" information. But if enough neurons are activated, this simple code can handle very complicated information. Scientists think that brain cells grow more synapses and put out new branches along busy message routes. These new connections form throughout our lives, and make up our memories.

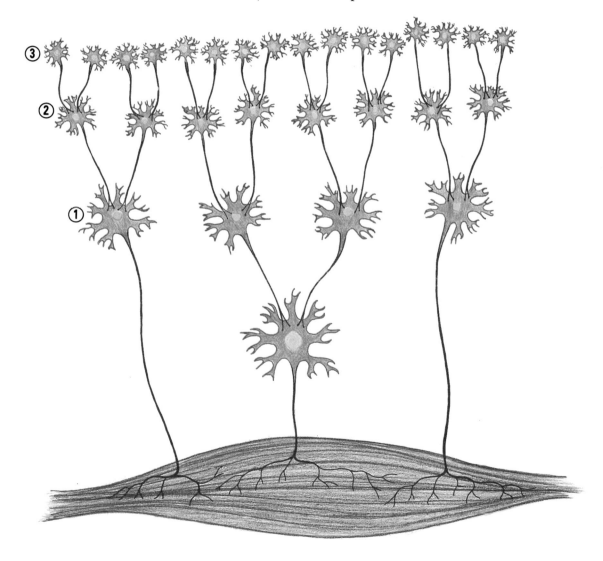

The upper brain

The upper and lower parts of our brain do different things. The upper brain, like the captain of a sports team, makes the important decisions. The lower brain is like the groundskeeper and his staff. Without them to keep the field in shape, there would be no game!

More than two thirds of our brain consists of the *cerebrum*. Only whales and dolphins have a larger cerebrum than humans. The crumpled surface of the cerebrum makes it look like a shelled walnut. By folding up the surface, a large number of cells can fit in a small space. If the surface were unfolded, it would have a total area of about half a square yard (half a square meter).

Our "thinking cap" is the *cerebral cortex*, which contains the tiny neurons which give us our intelligence and our skills.

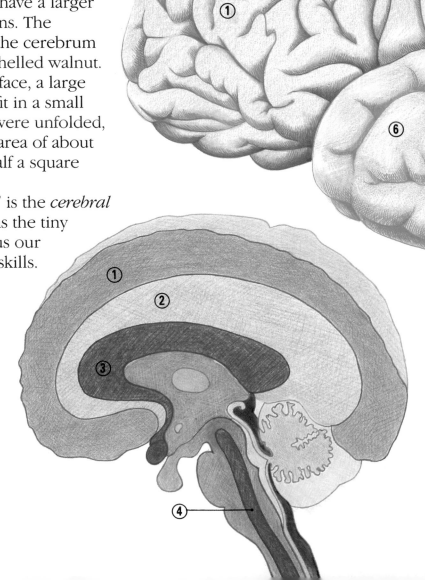

▶ A section through the brain. The front of the head is to the left and the back of the head to the right. We are looking at the inside of the right hemisphere of the brain.

① cerebral cortex, or gray matter
② white matter
③ corpus callosum
④ spinal cord

14

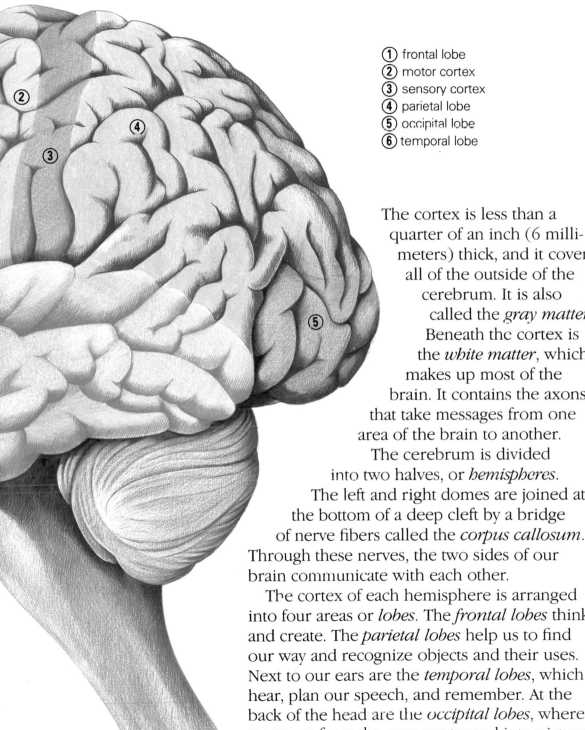

1 frontal lobe
2 motor cortex
3 sensory cortex
4 parietal lobe
5 occipital lobe
6 temporal lobe

The cortex is less than a quarter of an inch (6 millimeters) thick, and it covers all of the outside of the cerebrum. It is also called the *gray matter*. Beneath the cortex is the *white matter*, which makes up most of the brain. It contains the axons that take messages from one area of the brain to another.

The cerebrum is divided into two halves, or *hemispheres*. The left and right domes are joined at the bottom of a deep cleft by a bridge of nerve fibers called the *corpus callosum*. Through these nerves, the two sides of our brain communicate with each other.

The cortex of each hemisphere is arranged into four areas or *lobes*. The *frontal lobes* think and create. The *parietal lobes* help us to find our way and recognize objects and their uses. Next to our ears are the *temporal lobes*, which hear, plan our speech, and remember. At the back of the head are the *occipital lobes*, where messages from the eyes are turned into pictures.

The way we think

The left and right sides of our brain think very differently. Our left brain controls the right side of the body, and our right brain controls the left side. Normally they work together, but in some serious operations they have had to be divided, and it has been found that they can operate as separate "brains."

The left brain is good at the logical thinking we need for language and mathematics. Parts of the left brain control our speech and our ability to write. The right brain appreciates art and music and has a sense of space. It uses rhythms and colors, and is good at creative thinking. It is skillful at recognizing shapes and patterns. The right side of our brain will provide an immediate answer to a problem, whereas the left side will solve it in deliberate steps.

For us to function well, both brains must work in partnership. Leonardo da Vinci was a genius because he was both a great artist and a great scientist. Albert Einstein, the great physicist, was nearly thrown out of school because his teacher thought he couldn't do math, and because he was always daydreaming. These men used both halves of their brains to solve problems that no one had thought of before.

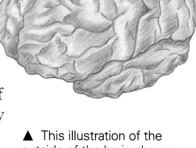

▲ This illustration of the outside of the brain shows the two hemispheres. They look like the two halves of a walnut. The front of the head is to the left.

▼ A section through the brain, looking toward the back. In this photo the gray matter shows up yellow and the white matter is brown.

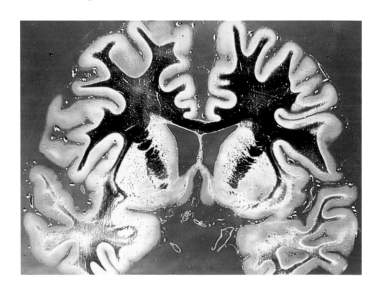

▲ The two sides of your face are controlled by different halves of your brain. Tension in the muscles driven by the two halves is different, so the muscles stretch differently. These pictures were made by cutting a photo of a face in half. (*left*) Right-hand side of the face, joined to its mirror image; (*middle*) normal face; (*right*) left-hand side joined to its mirror image.

▶You know whether you are left- or right-handed, but do you know if your left or right brain is dominant? Try holding a finger about 6 inches (15 centimeters) from your nose. Put a finger from your other hand 6 inches (15 centimeters) behind it. Now close one eye. Does one finger move right or left? Try again, closing the other eye. If the more distant finger vanishes when seen by the right eye, and moves left when seen by the left eye, you are "left-brained" – and vice versa.

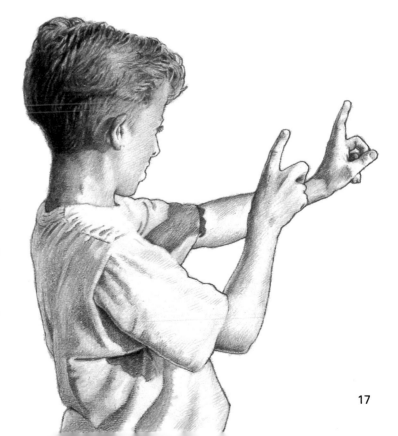

The "brainy" part of the cortex is the frontal lobes. The brain recognizes things in patterns. When we see an object, we identify it by matching it with images in our memory bank. When Charles Darwin, the famous naturalist, landed on Tierra del Fuego, the native Indians could not recognize his ship. They had no pattern of a ship in their minds!

▼ *Up and down,* an impossible figure by M. C. Escher (1898–1972), showing the same courtyard from the top and bottom of the stairs.

▲ Familiar objects can look different when seen close-up. Can you see what this picture shows?

Answer: colored pencils.

▲ How to make a Möbius strip.

Try this puzzle. Take a strip of paper about three feet (one meter) long and three inches (eight centimeters) wide. Draw an X on one side and an O on the other. Put a half turn in it and tape the ends together. You have made a Möbius strip. Now draw a continuous line from the X to the O. You will see that the shape you have made has only one surface. Next make a hole in the paper and cut along the line. You still have one strip! What do you think would happen if you did the same thing again?

Our right brain can understand the Möbius strip, but because it does not control speech, it cannot explain it. The left brain, which has the words, does not understand shapes, so it cannot explain it either.

As a detective sifts clues to find a criminal, so our left brain narrows patterns down to words. This is called *convergent thinking*. The right brain uses *divergent thinking*, in which we spread patterns out. For example, if you found an unfamiliar tool, your left brain would seek a word to describe it, while your right brain would think of how many different ways you might use it.

To be intelligent, we must think well. But an intelligence test which only checks our word and number skills is only testing half our brain. The practical skills of survival are as great, and need as much of our brain, as formal learning. For example, children living in a tropical rain forest might not be able to read and write. But they might be able to recognize many different kinds of bees, know which make honey, and know which are dangerous.

The lower brain

The lower brain is the control room for much of what we do automatically. It is also in charge of many of our life-support systems.

The *medulla*, or brain stem, connects the rest of the brain to the spinal cord. It is the switchboard for nerves to and from the body, especially nerves to the heart, lungs, and stomach. It controls our heartbeat, blood pressure, and breathing. The *midbrain* is a small part of the brain stem that contains many important nerve cells. Some such nerves control the muscles that move our eyes.

▲ The size of the lower brain varies between animals. A cat has a large cerebellum and an excellent sense of balance.

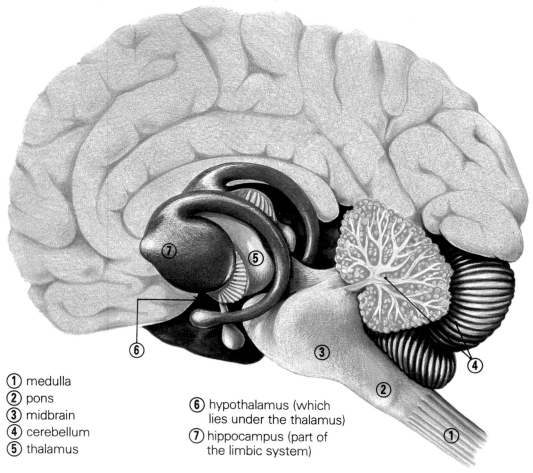

① medulla
② pons
③ midbrain
④ cerebellum
⑤ thalamus
⑥ hypothalamus (which lies under the thalamus)
⑦ hippocampus (part of the limbic system)

Above the medulla is the *pons*, which contains a timer that influences our waking and sleeping. Behind the brain stem is the *cerebellum*. It contains nearly as many neurons as the cortex, and coordinates our physical skills and controls our balance. It adjusts messages from the cortex to the nerves, and enables us to make delicate movements. Cats have a relatively large cerebellum, so they have excellent balance.

The *thalamus* deals with messages from our senses on their way to the cortex. It is also the brain's "panic button," preparing the body to escape if it senses pain. The *hypothalamus* keeps our body at the right temperature and tells us we need food or drink. The *limbic system* helps us to experience emotions, such as sadness or happiness. It is also important in memory. Although these things go on without our knowing, special training, such as yoga, can make us aware of some of them and even help us to control them.

▶ Yoga and meditation can help train our minds to be conscious of things we don't usually notice, such as breathing, heart rate, and muscle tension. This helps us to relax.

Sensation and movement

Two narrow strips across the cortex are responsible for registering our senses and for controlling our movements.

To survive we need to know what is touching us – is it hot, does it hurt? If we didn't know where our arms or legs were, or what they were doing, we might fall over. Sensory nerves run from our skin, muscles, and insides to our spinal cord. The messages they send through the spinal cord reach a part of the upper brain called the *sensory cortex*. Here, networks of brain cells deal with these messages all the time. Senses such as sight, hearing, touch, taste, and smell are so important that they have special brain areas of their own.

▼ This cutaway illustration shows the motor cortex of one hemisphere, and the sensory cortex of the other. Special brain areas deal with individual movements and senses.

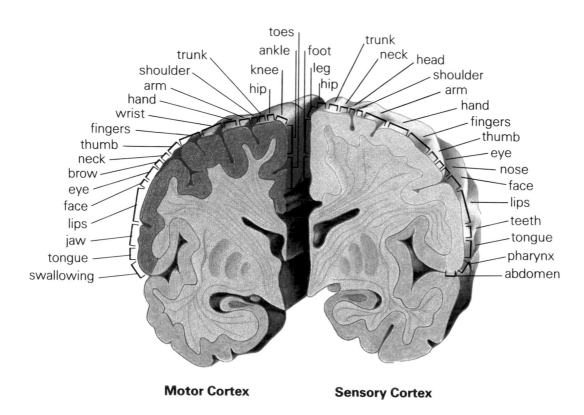

Motor Cortex   **Sensory Cortex**

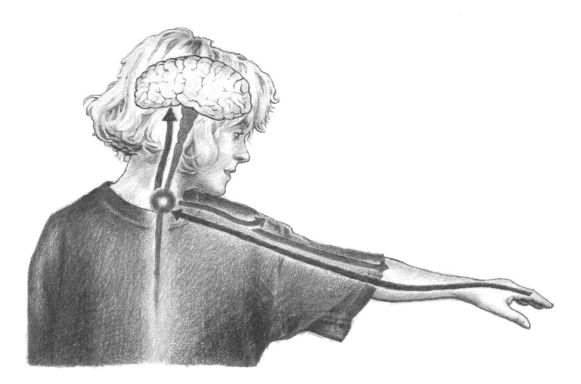

Planned movements are controlled by the *motor cortex*, which is next to the sensory cortex. Signals from the motor cortex are sent down nerves to our muscles. Delicate movements need more brain power than big ones, so our hands and lips have larger areas controlling them than our legs. When you learn a new skill, such as riding a bicycle, you are conscious of your motor cortex working. But once the pattern is learned, you no longer need to pay so much attention to how you do it. The pattern has become *unconscious*.

Sometimes we move before our brain has registered a sensory message. This is called a *reflex*. If we touch something hot, tiny sense organs in the skin, called *receptors*, send a warning signal along sensory nerves to the spinal cord. A response is triggered in the spinal cord, and a nerve activates a movement before the pain signal has reached our brain.

▲ If you touch a sharp pin, a message goes up a sensory nerve to your spinal cord. A motor nerve moves your hand away at once. A message goes to the brain, which knows about the pain after your hand has moved. Then the brain will move your eyes to look at what has happened.

Sleep

Now that you have gotten this far in the book, you may be feeling sleepy! If you fall asleep, will your brain go to sleep as well? If you don't dream, you may think it does. But in fact, the brain is as active at night as it is during the day. If you think you haven't dreamed during the night, you are probably wrong. You have just forgotten the dreams you had.

We spend about a third of our lives asleep. A baby needs at least 18 hours of sleep each day. Growing takes place only during our sleeping hours. As we grow less, we sleep less.

During sleep, the parts of our brain that control voluntary movements are at rest, but our reflexes are still at work. If a fly lands on our nose, we will brush it away, even if we are not aware of doing so.

When we first go to bed, we fall into a light, dreamless sleep. Our temperature and pulse rates drop. Because of the heat loss, we need blankets on our beds. About 90 minutes after we have fallen asleep, our breathing and pulse become irregular. Our ears are tuned for hearing and our eyes are moving rapidly. We are dreaming, imagining vivid scenes. Because our body is unable to move, nightmares are often about being chased, and not being able to escape, or falling off something and not being able to do anything about it. We spend about a quarter of the night in this kind of deep, dreaming sleep.

Brain Waves

waking

sleeping

dreaming

▲ The small amount of electricity your brain makes can be measured with special sensors. Patterns of fast, regular waves are found when we are awake. These may be to do with movements. They disappear in sleep, except when we are dreaming.

▼ Dreams can be analyzed, and their meaning can be interpreted. This is a real dream, originally told by a patient of the famous Swiss psychologist, Carl Jung (1875-1961).

All our brain clocks, including the one in the pons, are influenced by the limbic system. This is why worry and unhappiness keep us awake. Sleep is essential to good health. The brain probably uses dreams to sort out the events of the day.

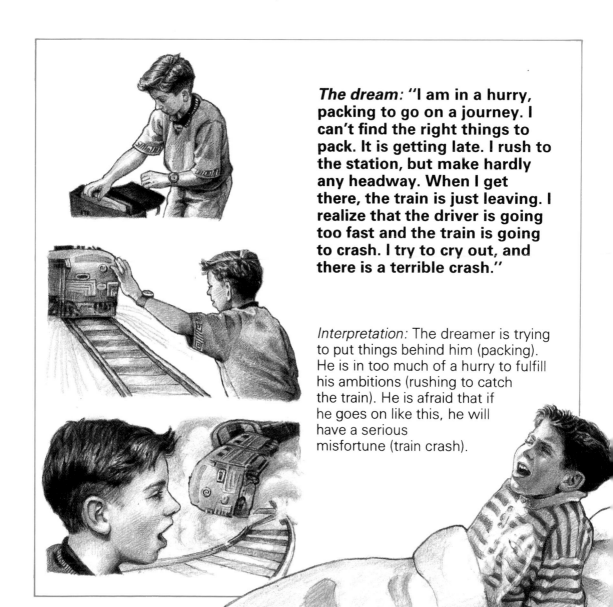

The dream: **"I am in a hurry, packing to go on a journey. I can't find the right things to pack. It is getting late. I rush to the station, but make hardly any headway. When I get there, the train is just leaving. I realize that the driver is going too fast and the train is going to crash. I try to cry out, and there is a terrible crash."**

Interpretation: The dreamer is trying to put things behind him (packing). He is in too much of a hurry to fulfill his ambitions (rushing to catch the train). He is afraid that if he goes on like this, he will have a serious misfortune (train crash).

Memory and learning

Learning depends on our ability to remember. Memories are stored when brain cells make new connections with each other. We know that memories are not just stored in one part of the cortex, because people who have suffered brain damage do not always lose their memory.

A memory is most likely to stick with us if it is very pleasant or very unpleasant. This is why the limbic system is so important to memory. It gives an "emotional label" to an event, which makes it easier to find among the billions of memories in our brain.

◄ Look at these objects for sixty seconds, then close the book and see how many objects you can remember. If you use spatial memory as well as visual memory, you will remember more. You could imagine walking along a street of shops – a bookshop, china shop, sports shop with a soccer ball and a baseball cap in the window, pet shop selling snakes, and so on.

◀ Mnemonics is a verse or sentence to help you remember things. You can remember the order of the colors of the rainbow by the first letters of the words in the sentence: "Richard of York gave battle in vain."

Sides of a ship: port=left (both words have the same number of letters).

The order of the planets in the solar system: "My very early morning jam sandwich usually nauseates people" (Mercury, Venus, Earth, Mars, Jupiter, Saturn, Uranus, Neptune, Pluto).

Ivan Pavlov, a Russian physiologist, studied the behavior of dogs. He found that if he rang a bell whenever he gave a dog food, the animal would eventually get excited just by the sound of a bell. We learn to like things if we connect them with a pleasant experience.

We have already seen that neurons spend more time switching off messages than switching them on. It has been estimated that the brain does not act on 99 percent of the information it receives. The reason for this is we concentrate on what interests us most at any particular time. We all know what it is like to forget something. In fact, the "forgotten" memory is still in our brain, but we don't know how to find it among our vast memory files. Hypnotists can often help people to remember things they thought they had forgotten.

Do you know the saying, "A picture is worth a thousand words"? We often remember a person's face, but forget his or her name. We can improve our memories with practice or by using tricks, such as putting letters into patterns.

Try studying the following 23 letters for 20 seconds:

PNTTVRIEOMMEIEOASRMRPSE

Now close the book and see how many of the letters you can remember and write down. If you get six, you are doing very well. On the next page you will find an easy way to do this exercise.

You will not even need 20 seconds to memorize the same letters now that we have re-ordered them:

PATTERNS IMPROVE MEMORIES

We add the things we learn to our memory. A young child has a lot of synapses to connect! This is why it is so important that children are surrounded by toys and books in their early years, and that they are talked to. If they have a lot of experiences in their memory when they go to school, learning will be easier.

When we begin to play a musical instrument, such as the violin, we find it difficult at first. Our brain has to learn how to instruct our fingers to make difficult movements. But regular practice programs our brain cells, and soon we find our fingers move easily. As we progress further, we no longer need to look at what we are doing. What we remember has become easy, and there is no end to what we can add to our music by learning.

▲ The Chinese written language is made up of picture symbols. Pictures have changed over the centuries, such as this one for "tiger."

◀ Road signs and ancient Sumerian writing also use pictures that can be recognized and remembered easily.

◄Peter Szumowski's painting, *The Neolithic Totem*, puts familiar things into a strange pattern. A totem is a symbol, and we use symbols to communicate things we cannot say with words. They can mean feelings, thoughts, or memories.

▼ Albert Einstein (1879–1955), the famous scientist, nearly got thrown out of school for "day-dreaming." In fact, he was probably practicing thinking in symbols. He did this so well that he solved many mysteries of the universe.

Most good artists learn by copying what other artists have done. They practice until they have mastered the skills of their craft. Great artists are creative. They discover new ways of expressing themselves. To do this, they need to have developed both their right and left brains to their fullest potential.

After Albert Einstein died, his brain was removed. He had asked scientists to study it after his death to see if his genius could be explained by anything abnormal. Scientists could find nothing unusual about the great man's brain. Our brain is what we make of it.

Glossary

arachnoid   the middle layer of the brain's three meninges coverings.

axon   a long extension from a neuron, carrying a message to another part of the body.

blood vessel   a tube carrying blood from one part of the body to another.

cell   the smallest single part of a living organism.

cell membrane   the outer surface of a cell.

central nervous system   the brain and spinal cord.

cerebellum   the part at the back of the brain that controls balance and fine movement.

cerebral cortex   the outer layer of the cerebrum, containing the gray matter.

cerebrum   the main part of the human brain, made up of two hemispheres.

convergent thinking   the kind of analytical thinking used in science, math, and by detectives — putting things together to find a single answer.

corpus callosum   the part of the brain that carries nerve fibers from one hemisphere to the other.

cytoplasm   the living contents of a cell, excluding the nucleus.

dendrite   a branched, threadlike extension of a neuron that carries signals to and from other neurons.

divergent thinking   the kind of creative thinking that goes from one idea to another and gives several possible solutions to a problem.

dura mater   the leathery outer covering of the brain.

frontal lobe   the front part of the brain, that does the most complicated thinking.

glia   cells that support and feed the neurons in the brain.

gray matter   a layer of the cerebrum containing mostly neurons.

hemisphere   one of the halves of the cerebrum.

hypothalamus   the part of the brain that regulates body temperature and other functions.

limbic system   part of the brain concerned with emotions.

lobe   one of the four areas of the cerebral cortex (the frontal, parietal, temporal, and occipital lobes).

macrophage   a cell that clears up dead cells and kills germs.

medulla   the stalklike section where the brain and spinal cord join; it is a large switching station for nerves from and to the body.

membrane   a thin sheet of tissue, usually holding things in; for example, a cell membrane.

meninges   the three membranes that cover the brain (dura mater, arachnoid, and pia mater).

midbrain   part of the brain stem above the medulla.

mitochondria   energy-making structures in a cell.

motor cortex   the part of the upper brain that controls the body's movements.

myelin   fatty tissue that forms a covering around axons.

nerve   a bundle of fibers, carrying messages between the brain and other parts of the body.

neuron   a nerve cell.

nucleus   the central compartment of a cell that contains the DNA (which contains instructions for making all the chemicals the cell produces).

occipital lobe   part of the brain at the back of the head, concerned with sight.

parietal lobe   part of the brain at the side, helping us to find our way and recognize objects and their uses.

pia mater   the soft inner covering of the brain.

pons   part of the brain above the medulla and below the thalamus, carrying nerves up to and down from the brain.

receptor   a sense organ in the skin.

reflex   a response of the body, usually to something painful, that causes avoiding action to take place, without the brain being involved.

sensory cortex   the part of the upper brain where sensations are dealt with.

spinal cord   the column of nerve fibers running to and from the brain down the middle of the backbone.

synapse   the place where two neurons meet.

temporal lobe   the part of the brain concerned with hearing, speech, and memory.

thalamus   the innermost part of the brain, where pain is felt.

unconscious   not aware of one's actions; the unconscious comprises all the things in our brain that we are not paying attention to at any moment.

white matter   part of the brain beneath the cerebral cortex, containing mostly axons.

Index